A YouTuber's Cooking Playlist

Nicole Burgess

50 Shades of Mom – Kiera Avery

LemonadeMom – Vanessa Lemon

ISBN: 9781726745598
Imprint: Independently Published

Table of Contents

Our Beach Menu

50 Shades of Mom 12

Table of Contents (cont.)

Tropical Parfait
Nicole Burgess

32 oz vanilla Greek yogurt
1 pint of strawberries
Pineapple tidbits
Mango chunks
Toasted coconut

Directions

1. In cups, layer the yogurt, fruit, more yogurt and top with more fruit and the toasted coconut.
2. Place plastic wrap on top of each cup and store for an easy breakfast all week!

Crustless Quiche Lorraine
LemonadeMom

8 turkey bacon slices, cooked & chopped
1 cup shredded Swiss cheese
1 medium onion, diced
2 Tbsp flour
4 eggs
1 cup milk
1/8 tsp cayenne pepper
Salt & pepper to taste

Directions

3. Heat oven to 350 degrees.
4. Lightly grease a 9-inch pie plate.
5. Toss the bacon, cheese, onion and flour together and spread in the bottom of the pie plate.
6. In a bowl, beat the eggs together first, then beat in milk and add seasonings.
7. Pour egg mixture over bacon mixture.
8. Bake uncovered for 40 minutes.
9. Let stand 10 minutes before cutting.

Pineapple Mimosa Punch
50 Shades of Mom

1 can of Dole pineapple juice
1 (64 oz) container of orange juice
1 bottle of champagne

Directions

1. Mix all ingredients together.
2. Serve chilled & garnish with fresh strawberries.

Monte Cristos
50 Shades of Mom

1 loaf of challah bread
1 cup milk
5 eggs
2 Tbsp vanilla
2 Tbsp cinnamon
1/2 lb honey turkey
1/2 lb honey ham
10 slices of Swiss cheese

Directions

1. Mix milk, eggs, cinnamon and vanilla together.
2. Slice bread about one inch thick.
3. Dunk and fully coat bread in milk mixture and brown on both sides in a buttered frying pan.
4. When all bread has been browned, place a piece back in the pan one at a time.
5. Top that bread with 2 slices of turkey, 2 slices of ham, and 2 slices of Swiss cheese.
6. Add another piece of bread on top.
7. Cook for about 2 minutes and flip over adding more butter to the bottom of the pan.
8. Cook for 2 more minutes or until warm in the center and melty.
9. Repeat until there are no ingredients left.
10. Serve with maple syrup and mayo.

Cheeseburger Sliders
Nicole Burgess

2 lbs ground meat
1 small onion, chopped
1/2 cup BBQ sauce
1/4 cup bread crumbs
1/2 Tbsp seasoned salt
1/2 tsp garlic powder
6 slices of cheese (I use Velveeta slices)
12 slider rolls (I use Cobblestone party rolls)
Pepper to taste

Directions

1. Preheat oven to 400 degrees.
2. In a bowl, combine ground meat, onion, breadcrumbs, BBQ sauce, seasoned salt, garlic powder and pepper.
3. Press the meat mixture into a 9x13 pan making a huge hamburger patty.
4. Poke holes in the meat with a fork for even cooking.
5. Bake for 30 minutes.
6. Once the meat is done cooking, drain off excess grease.
7. Place the sliced cheese on top of the meat and return to the oven for a few minutes or until cheese melts.
8. Hold a slider over the meat to gauge the size to cut the burgers. Serve with pickle slices, mayo, BBQ sauce, etc.

My Favorite Chicken Salad
LemonadeMom

1 rotisserie chicken (about 3-4 cups of cooked, shredded chicken)
1 cup of seedless grapes, sliced in half (I use a mixture of red and green)
1 cup almonds, thinly sliced
1 celery stalk, sliced
4 green onions, thinly sliced, end to end
2 Tbsp fresh dill, chopped
1 Tbsp fresh parsley, chopped
1 cup mayo
Juice of 1 lemon
1 Tbsp Dijon mustard
Salt & pepper to taste

Directions

1. In a large bowl, mix together the chicken, grapes, almonds, celery, green onions, dill and parsley.
2. In a small bowl, mix together the mayo, lemon, mustard, salt and pepper.
3. Add mayo mixture to chicken mixture and gently stir until mixed well.
4. Refrigerate for at least one hour.

Buffalo Chicken Dip
50 Shades of Mom

2 (10 oz) cans or 2 cups of cooked, shredded chicken
1 block of cream cheese, softened
1/2 cup of mozzarella cheese
1/2 cup of crumbled blue cheese
1/2 cup of Ranch dressing
1/2 cup of blue cheese dressing
1/2 cup of hot sauce

Directions

1. Add all ingredients into a large mixing bowl until well combined.
2. Place in an oven safe dish and bake at 350 degrees for 20 minutes or until hot all the way through.

Mom's Crawfish Dip
Nicole Burgess

2 sticks butter
2 lbs of crawfish tails
2 cans cream of mushroom soup
1 bunch of green onions, chopped
1 yellow onion, chopped
2 dashes of liquid crab boil
Garlic powder to taste
Salt & pepper to taste

Directions

1. Sauté onions with butter.
2. Add crawfish tails and remaining ingredients.
3. Let cook, slow, stirring occasionally for 30 minutes.
4. Serve with your favorite crackers. I suggest Melba Toast Rounds.

Fresh Salsa
LemonadeMom

6 large tomatoes, diced
4 fresh jalapeno peppers, diced
1 green bell pepper, diced
1 bunch of green onions, chopped end to end
1 Tbsp chili powder
1 Tbsp garlic salt
3-4 Tbsp cilantro, chopped
1 tsp salt
1 tsp pepper
2 Tbsp canola oil
Pinch of oregano

Directions

1. Mix all ingredients together and chill in fridge for 1 hour.

Slow Cooker Cola Ribs
Nicole Burgess

1 rack of ribs
1 can of cola
Cajun seasoning to taste
1.5 cups of BBQ sauce
1 slow cooker liner
Salt & pepper to taste

Directions

1. Place your slow cooker liner in your slow cooker.
2. Season both sides of your ribs.
3. Place the ribs in the slow cooker.
4. Pour the cola over the ribs.
5. Cook on low for 8-10 hours.
6. Once ribs are done, carefully take out and place on an aluminum foil lined sheet pan.
7. Lather your ribs with the BBQ sauce.
8. Place under a broiler until the sauce starts to caramelize.
9. Remove from the oven.

Texas Baked Beans
LemonadeMom

1 Tbsp butter
1 Tbsp olive oil
2 cloves garlic, minced
1 red onion, diced
1 lb bacon, diced
3 jalapenos, seeded and diced
1 red bell pepper, diced
1 bottle of beer (I use Blue Moon)
1 cup BBQ sauce
1/2 cup brown sugar
1/4 cup molasses
6 cups canned pinto beans, drained
Salt to taste

Directions

1. Preheat oven to 375 degrees.
2. In a large sauté pan, heat the oil and butter.
3. Cook the garlic and onions until soft.
4. Add all the peppers and cook until soft.
5. Cook bacon separately until crispy and set aside.
6. In a large bowl combine the beer, BBQ sauce, brown sugar and molasses.
7. Add the beans, peppers and half the bacon.
8. Season with salt.
9. Transfer to a 9x13 baking dish, sprinkle other half of bacon on top and bake for 45 minutes.

Cheddar & Bacon Potato Salad
50 Shades of Mom

2.5 lbs red potatoes, cut into chunks
1 cup shredded cheddar cheese
1/2 cup bacon crumbles
1/4 cup green onion, diced
1 cup mayo
1/2 cup ranch
1/2 cup sour cream
Salt & pepper to taste

Directions

1. Boil potatoes until fork tender in salted water.
2. Drain and let cool.
3. Add all remaining ingredients to fully cooled potatoes.
4. Mix thoroughly.

Mom's Cheesecake
50 Shades of Mom

4 eggs
1 cup sugar
1 Tbsp corn starch
28 oz cream cheese, softened
1/2 cup heavy cream
2 cups sour cream
1 Tbsp vanilla extract
1 tsp almond extract
Graham cracker crumbs

Directions

1. Beat eggs until thick.
2. Add sugar and cornstarch and mix.
3. Add cream cheese and mix.
4. Add heavy cream and sour cream and mix.
5. Add all extracts and mix well.
6. Pour into a spring form pan lined with graham cracker crumbs.
7. Bake at 375 degrees for 45 minutes.
8. Chill before serving.

Strawberry Shortcake Trifle
Nicole Burgess

1 angel food cake (store bought or made)
12 oz frozen whipped topping, thawed
For the cream:
8 oz cream cheese, softened
14 oz can condensed milk
12 oz frozen whipped topping, thawed
For the strawberry glaze:
1 cup sugar
3 Tbsp cornstarch
3 Tbsp strawberry gelatin
1 cup water
2 cups diced strawberries

Directions

1. In a mixer, mix the cream cheese, milk and whipped topping.
2. Set aside.
3. In a saucepan, stir the sugar, cornstarch and gelatin together.
4. Add water.
5. Cook stirring over low-medium heat until thickened.
6. Remove from heat and allow to cool completely.
7. Once cooled, fold in your diced strawberries.
8. In a trifle bowl, layer your cut, chunked angel food cake, strawberry glaze, cream.
9. Repeat in this order until out of ingredients.
10. Use your other 12 oz container of whipped topping for the top of the trifle bowl.
11. Place a few strawberries on top for garnish.

Buttermilk Pound Cake
LemonadeMom

3 cups flour
1/2 tsp baking soda
1/2 tsp baking powder
1/2 tsp salt
2 sticks butter
1/2 cup vegetable shortening
3 cups sugar
5 eggs
1/2 Tbsp vanilla extract
1/2 Tbsp almond extract
1 cup buttermilk

Directions

1. Preheat oven to 325 degrees.
2. Grease and flour a 10" bundt pan.
3. Sift together the flour, baking soda, baking powder and salt. Set aside.
4. Using an electric mixer, cream the butter, shortening and sugar until fluffy.
5. Add the eggs one at a time and mix well after each.
6. Add the dry ingredients and buttermilk alternately to the butter mixture, beginning and ending with the flour.
7. Add the extracts and mix well.
8. Pour batter into bundt pan.
9. Bake for 1 hour and 45 minutes.
10. Remove from oven and let cool in pan for 10 minutes.
11. Invert into a cake plate.
12. Serve with strawberries and whipped cream.

50 Shades of MOM

Hey guys! Kiera here from 50 Shades of Mom. I'm so excited about this cookbook, you have no idea. If this is the first time meeting me, let me tell you a little bit about myself.

I'm a Long Island born and raised Italian girl, who relocated her family, then just a small crowd of three, to the good ole' south. South Carolina to be exact. I've spent most of my life in the restaurant business, from waiting tables to serving up drinks, but my true passion comes from being in the kitchen. Food will always proudly be my first love. I do have some other loves of my life that snuck in my heart and refuse to leave, and that is my husband who I've been with for 14 years, and our three beautiful children, Jacob, Mason, and Maya. I've been lucky enough to be their full time stay at home mommy for the last five years, and there isn't a thing I would change about our world.

Although I enjoyed the busy bustle of the restaurant life, this time at home has given me a chance to hone in on perfecting recipes and experimenting with new ones. My goal in life is to one day open a restaurant, but I see that in the future when life slows down a bit. In the meantime, being home has also allowed me to start my YouTube channel, which in turn has given me an opportunity to still share my recipes with you all, but most importantly, has allowed me to meet these amazing ladies I'm writing this book with. I'm loving this ride so much and hope you all are enjoying coming along with us.

Cream Corn

4 oz cream cheese, room temp
2 cups corn
1/2 stick butter, softened
1/4 cup sugar
1 cup heavy cream
Pepper to taste

Directions

1. Over medium heat, add the butter and cream cheese to a saucepan and stir constantly until the two are incorporated together.
2. Slowly add the heavy cream and stir until smooth.
3. Now mix in the sugar and corn.
4. Cook on low and simmer for 30-40 minutes or until desired consistency.
5. The longer it sits the creamier it will be.

Cheesy Bacon Chicken

2 lbs thinly sliced chicken cutlets
10 slices of bacon
8 oz cream cheese, softened
1 cup shredded cheddar cheese
1 cup diced green onion
Salt & pepper to taste

Directions

1. Mix together cream cheese, shredded cheese and green onion in a bowl and set aside.
2. Lightly salt and pepper each side of your chicken cutlets and lay them flat on a cutting board.
3. Spoon some of the cream cheese onto the chicken.
4. Starting at one end roll the chicken into a log.
5. Take a slice of bacon and begin wrapping it around the chicken until it's completely covered.
6. Place seam side down on a baking sheet and bake at 350 degrees for 35 minutes.

Meat Sauce

2 (28 oz) cans tomato sauce
1 small can tomato paste
1.5 lbs ground meat (sausage, beef, or a mixture of both)
2 Tbsp olive oil
1 small onion, diced
1 small head of garlic, diced
1 Tbsp basil
3 Tbsp parmesan cheese
2 Tbsp garlic powder
1 tsp onion powder
1.5 tsp oregano
3 Tbsp sugar
2 bay leaves
Salt & pepper to taste

Directions

1. Heat oil in sauce pot.
2. When oil has reached sizzle, add in onions and garlic and sauté until lightly brown.
3. When the onions and garlic are done, add in your meat and cook until brown.
4. Once the meat is brown, add the sauce, making sure to add water to the cans so you get all the sauce in the pot, including about 14 oz of water.
5. Stir well.
6. Add in all of your other ingredients, except for the paste, and let simmer on low heat for 90 minutes.
7. Add in paste and full can of paste water and stir well.
8. Let sit another 30 minutes.
9. Fish out your bay leaves and you are good to go.

Italian Meatballs

1.5 lbs ground beef
2 eggs
3/4 cup milk
1/2 cup parmesan cheese
1 cup Italian seasoned breadcrumbs
1 Tbsp garlic powder
1 tsp onion powder
1 tsp salt
1.5 tsp pepper

Directions

1. Mix all ingredients together. It's ok to dive in and get your hands dirty.
2. Continue to mix until well combined.
3. Roll the meat mixture into your desired size balls.
4. Place on a cookie sheet lined with wax paper and bake in a 350 degree oven for 20-25 minutes or until cooked thoroughly.

Pot Pies

2 cups of cooked chicken, chopped
1 cup chopped onion
1 cup chopped celery
2 cups frozen mixed veggies (I use the peas/carrots/corn blend)
1/3 cup butter
1/2 cup flour
2 cups chicken broth
1 tsp salt
1 tsp pepper
4 unbaked pie crusts

Directions

1. Sauté onion, celery and veggies in the butter over medium heat for about 3-5 minutes or until all veggies are tender.
2. Add the flour and stir for one minute or until smooth.
3. Now add the liquids and keep stirring until the milk and broth are thickened and bubbly.
4. Stir in chicken, salt and pepper and mix well.
5. Let cool completely before pouring into pie crusts.
6. Roll out your pie dough and place your bottoms in both pans. Pour the filling into your crusts and divide evenly.
7. Use your remaining crusts to cover your mixture.
8. Fold the edges over the sides and use a fork to seal the edges.
9. Poke holes with a fork or cut a slit with a knife into the top of the pies after sealing. It allows the hot air to escape and not explode your beautiful pies.
10. Bake at 375 degrees for 30-45 minutes or until pie crust is golden brown. Let stand 10 minutes before serving.

Chicken Roll-ups

3 boneless chicken breasts, cubed
3 colored peppers, diced
1 small onion, diced
1/2 cup of frozen corn
5 oz cream cheese
1 cup shredded cheddar or Mexican blend cheese
1 cup mozzarella cheese
3 oz of Velveeta (optional)
3 Tbsp olive oil
Cooking spray
Garlic powder, chili powder and cumin to taste

Directions

1. Sauté chicken, peppers and onion in a frying pan with olive oil. Salt and pepper to taste. Cook thoroughly.
2. While the chicken is cooking, place all cheeses, frozen corn and seasoning into a mixing bowl.
3. Add hot chicken mixture to bowl and stir until creamy.
4. Add cooking spray to already used frying pan. Reheat pan to medium heat.
5. Roll chicken mixture in tortillas and place in frying pan.
6. Cook 3 minutes or until golden brown on each side.
7. Serve with sour cream and salsa.

Instant Pot Coconut Rice

2 cups basmati rice
2 cups coconut water
1 can full fat coconut milk
1/4 cup sweetened shredded coconut
Salt & pepper to taste

Directions

1. Pour the rice, coconut water, coconut milk and shredded coconut into the Instant Pot.
2. Close the lid and set on white rice setting.
3. Once the Instant Pot has finished cooking, allow it to slow release for 15 minutes.
4. Quick release the remaining pressure and remove the lid.
5. Fluff rice with a fork and season with desired salt and pepper.

Strawberry Basil Chicken with Balsamic Glaze

2 lbs thin sliced chicken cutlets
2 cups diced strawberries
1 cup diced basil
3 Tbsp olive oil
3 Tbsp balsamic glaze *Instructions below
4 cloves diced garlic
Salt & pepper to taste

Directions

1. Thin slice your chicken and salt/pepper on both sides.
2. Brush with olive oil and cook thoroughly on the grill.
3. While the chicken is on the grill, mix together strawberries, basil, 1 Tbsp of olive oil and the balsamic glaze.
4. Once the chicken is cooked through, add tablespoons of olive oil and garlic to a pan and heat until warm.
5. Once you smell that fragrant garlic, add the chicken and just sauté 1-2 minutes on each side to absorb the garlic flavor.
6. Place the cooked chicken on a plate and ladle the strawberry mixture over the chicken. Add some extra balsamic glaze and serve hot.

Balsamic Glaze

1.5 cups balsamic vinegar
1.5 tsp honey

Directions

1. Bring both ingredients to a boil on the stove and reduce the heat down to a simmer.
2. Stirring occasionally, continue to simmer until the pot has reduced down to half its size.
3. Remove from the heat and allow to cool completely.

Pineapple Bacon Burgers

1 lb ground beef
8 slices of bacon
4 pineapple slices
Salt & pepper to taste

Directions

1. Add a generous amount of salt and pepper to your ground beef and mix well.
2. Form the ground beef into 4 hamburger patties and set aside.
3. Precook the bacon on a cookie sheet in a 325 degree oven for 10 minutes. You still want bacon to be pliable.
4. Place on a paper towel to drip dry and cool.
5. Once bacon is cool, lay it in an X formation.
6. Place your burger patty in the center of the X.
7. Add the pineapple slice on top.
8. Fold the bacon over the pineapple.
9. Grill until bacon and burger are to your desired doneness.

Stuffed Flank Steak

4-6 lbs of flank steak
2 cups fresh spinach
4-6 slices provolone cheese
1 cup shredded mozzarella cheese
2 sheets wax paper
Meat tenderizer
Salt & pepper to taste

Directions

1. Take your steak and place it between 2 sheets of wax paper.
2. Use the meat tenderizer and flatten the steak to no more than 1/4 of an inch thick.
3. Generously season your steak with salt and pepper.
4. Sprinkle the mozzarella cheese onto the steak and spread it evenly.
5. Now add the layer of spinach on top of the mozzarella.
6. Finally place the slices of provolone on top of the spinach layer.
7. Starting at one end roll the steak as tightly as possible so the insides don't fall out.
8. Once it's rolled tightly, slice 1-inch slices and place them on a foil lined cookie sheet that's sprayed with cooking spray.
9. Cook for 20 minutes on 350 degrees or until an internal temp of 160 degrees.

Taco Soup

1.5 lbs ground beef
32 oz beef broth
10 oz pineapple salsa
1 can red kidney beans
1 can pinto beans
1 cup corn
2 pets taco seasoning
1.5 Tbsp chili powder
1 small onion
3 cloves garlic

Directions

1. Add ground beef to a frying pan on medium heat and brown, mixing occasionally until all the pink is gone and the meat is cooked throughout.
2. Add the browned ground beef and remaining ingredients to the crockpot and cook for 4 hours on high or 8 hours on low.

Chicken Marsala

2 lbs chicken breast, thinly sliced
1 lb portobello mushroom, chopped
32 oz chicken stock
1/3 lb prosciutto, chopped
1/3 bottle sweet marsala wine
4 cloves garlic, chopped
1 small onion, diced
1/2 cup olive oil
1/4 cup flour plus extra for coating chicken

Directions

1. Add oil to frying pan and bring up to medium heat.
2. Coat thinly sliced chicken with flour.
3. Place in oil when heated and cook until golden brown.
4. Place cooked chicken off to the side.
5. In the same pan sauté mushrooms, onions, prosciutto and garlic until the vegetables are tender.
6. Add broth and flour and stir until smooth.
7. Add marsala wine and cook for 10 minutes to ensure all alcohol has burned off.
8. Add chicken back to the pan and cook for another 10 minutes on medium to low heat.
9. Serve over pasta.

Enchiladas

2 lbs ground beef
8 large flour tortillas
2 (10 oz) cans enchilada sauce
1 cup diced onions
1 cup diced peppers
1.5 cups shredded cheese
1 can of your favorite beans

Directions

1. Heat skillet on medium, adding 2 Tbsp of olive oil.
2. When sizzling, add onions, peppers and beans.
3. Once vegetables are tender and cooked through, about 10 minutes, add in ground beef.
4. Once the meat is brown all the way through add in one can of enchilada sauce.
5. Cook the sauce and the meat until most of the fluid is absorbed into the meat.
6. Mix in one cup of cheese until melted.
7. Set aside for 10 minutes to congeal.
8. Spoon 2 large spoonfuls of meat mixture in the center of the tortillas and roll like a cigar.
9. Place them seam side down in a greased 9x13 pan.
10. Drizzle last can of enchilada sauce over tortillas and sprinkle remaining cheese on top.
11. Bake in a 350 degree oven for 10 minutes or until cheese is melted.
12. Serve warm with sour cream.

Alla Vodka Sauce

28 oz can tomato sauce
1 small can tomato paste
1 cup prosciutto, diced
4 oz vodka
1 small onion, diced
4 cloves garlic, minced
1/2 cup parmesan cheese
12 oz heavy cream
3 Tbsp olive oil
3 pieces fresh basil

Directions

1. Warm olive oil in a large skillet on medium heat.
2. Sauté onions, garlic and prosciutto until slightly brown.
3. Turn pan up to high heat.
4. Add vodka.
5. Stir until almost all liquid is cooked away.
6. Add tomato sauce and heat until bubbling.
7. Add parmesan cheese. Stir until cheese dissolves.
8. Add heavy cream a little at a time and stir until it's mixed thoroughly.
9. Add tomato paste with one can of water and stir again until paste is completely dissolved.
10. Simmer on low for 10-15 minutes.
11. Yields enough for one pound of pasta.

Pineapple Upside Down Cake

1 box of pineapple cake mix (you will need the ingredients and to prepare as directed)
1 can pineapple slices
2 sticks butter
1.5 cups light brown sugar
8 maraschino cherries

Directions

1. Prepare box mix as directed and set aside.
2. Melt butter in a microwaveable bowl.
3. Pour the butter evenly between 2 cake pans.
4. Add brown sugar to the pans, again dividing evenly between both pans.
5. Using a fork, or your hands, pat the brown sugar into an even layer covering the entire bottom of the pans.
6. Add 4 pineapple slices on top of the brown sugar. Side by side 2x2. Do this on both pans.
7. Cut a sliver off the back of the cherries.
8. Place the cherries cut side up one in the middle of each pineapple ring.
9. Pour cake mix, dividing evenly into each cake pan.
10. Bake as directed on the box.
11. Once cooked and cooled, flip one cake pan onto a plate and then flip the other cake on top.
12. Viola, double layer pineapple upside down cake.

Hey guys! My name is Vanessa, aka LemonadeMom. I am so excited to share this cookbook with you.

My cooking style is all over the place. Growing up with both parents in the military, trying all kinds of new and foreign foods, I cook just about everything. I have been happily married for the past 8 years and have 4 beautiful children, Paige, Bryce, Rose and Pearl. I love creating and molding recipes into dishes my family will enjoy. I have to thank my mother for my love of cooking. She is the best cook I know and I love eating what she comes up with in her kitchen.

As a stay-at-home mom, I started my YouTube channel to break out of my mom rut. I have met so many amazing people, including Kiera and Nicole. It really has changed my life and made me realize just how much I love being in the kitchen. I hope you love these recipes as much as I do.

Grown Up Watermelon Lemonade

5 cups seedless watermelon, cubed
1 (12 ounce) can frozen lemonade
1 3/4 cups water
1 1/4 cups vodka
Ice
Lemon slice (optional garnish)

Directions

1. Add ice, watermelon and lemonade to blender.
2. Blend until mixed and the consistency you want.
3. Pour into a pitcher.
4. Stir in water and vodka.

Whole Wheat Pumpkin Waffles

1/4 cup melted butter
2.5 cups whole wheat flour
2 tsp baking soda
1 tsp baking powder
1/2 tsp salt
1.5 tsp cinnamon
1/2 tsp cloves
1 tsp nutmeg
1/2 big can of pumpkin
4 eggs
2 cups milk

Directions

1. Combine all dry ingredients in a large bowl.
2. Make a large well in the center.
3. Add wet ingredients to well and start whisking together.
4. When well combined, cook according to waffle iron directions.

Spicy Crackers

4 sleeves saltine crackers
1 1/3 cup canola oil
2 Tbsp red pepper flakes
1 tsp garlic powder
1 pkg Ranch dressing mix

Directions

1. Pour saltines in a 1-gallon bag.
2. Mix oil and seasonings together in a small bowl.
3. Pour mixture over crackers.
4. Close bag and turn onto a new side every 15 minutes for 2 hours to evenly distribute.

Cowboy Caviar

1/2 cup olive oil
1/3 cup sugar
1/3 cup white wine vinegar
1 tsp chili powder
1 tsp salt
1 lb Roma tomatoes, seeded and diced
1 (15 ounce) can black-eyed peas, rinsed and drained
1 (15 ounce) can black beans, rinsed and drained
1 (15 ounce) can super sweet corn, drained
1 red onion, diced
1 green bell Pepper, diced
1 red bell pepper, diced
1 bunch cilantro, chopped

Directions

1. In a large bowl, mix together the olive oil, sugar, white wine vinegar, chili powder, and salt.
2. Add tomatoes, black-eyed peas, black beans, corn, red onion, and both bell peppers to bowl.
3. Stir to combine.
4. Stir in cilantro.
5. Cover and chill 1 hour or even overnight to blend flavors.

Summer Fruit Salad

1 cantaloupe
1 basket of blueberries
2 sprigs of basil
4 oz sugar
1/2 bottle of sweet white wine (I suggest Dulcis Moscato D'asti)
4 peaches
1 basket of strawberries
1 sprig of mint
1 tsp vanilla

Directions

1. Peel the cantaloupe and dice all the fruit.
2. Mix gently with the sugar.
3. Thinly slice the mint and basil.
4. Pour the wine on the fruit.
5. Put in fridge to chill for 1/2 hour.

Artisan Baked Bread

3 cups all-purpose flour
1 tsp salt
1/2 tsp yeast
1.5 cups warm water

Directions

1. In a bowl, stir all ingredients until combined.
2. Cover with plastic wrap and leave at room temperature for 8 to 24 hours.
3. Turn dough out onto a well-floured surface and form into a ball.
4. Let it sit for 30 minutes.
5. In the meantime, place a baking dish with high sides (or Dutch Oven) into the oven and preheat it to 450 degrees.
6. Slash a X on top of the dough ball.
7. Carefully transfer dough to baking dish and cover with foil.
8. Bake for 30 minutes.
9. Uncover and bake an additional 10-15 minutes until golden brown.
10. Cool before slicing.

Banana Bread

1/2 cup canola oil
2 cups sugar
2 cups flour
1/2 cup chopped pecans (optional)
1/2 cup chocolate chips (optional)
1 tsp baking soda
3 over-ripe bananas, mashed
1 tsp salt
2 eggs

Directions

1. Mix each ingredient together in order. Meaning, mix the oil and sugar together, then add the flour and mix that, then add the optional ingredients and so on until it is all well combined.
2. Pour batter into a greased pan.
3. Bake at 350 degrees for 1 hour and 15 minutes (if baking as muffins, bake for 30-40 minutes).

Pasta Salad

1 box bowtie pasta
1 can small artichokes, cut in quarters
1 English cucumber, chopped
1 pkg cherub tomatoes, cut in half
1 bunch green onions, chopped
1 can small black olives, drained
3 pkgs Knorr Salat Kronung
3 Tbsp olive oil
McCormick Italian Herbs Grinder

Directions

1. Cook pasta (al dente).
2. Add all ingredients except Knorr pkgs, olive oil, and seasoning to a bowl.
3. In a small bowl add the Knorr pkgs, olive oil and 3 Tbsp water.
4. Whisk together then add to large bowl.
5. Add seasoning to taste and mix all together.

Fresh Corn-Rice Salad

4 ears fresh corn
2 cups cooked rice, cooled
2 cups cherub tomatoes, cut in half
1 small pkg baby spinach
1 red onion, diced
2 Tbsp rice vinegar
2 Tbsp olive oil
Salt & pepper to taste

Directions

1. Husk corn and remove silk.
2. Cook corn in boiling, lightly salted water for 3 minutes.
3. Remove and drain, then set aside to cool.
4. In a medium bowl, combine the cooled rice, tomatoes, spinach, and onion.
5. Cut corn off the cob and add to salad.
6. Mix everything to together then drizzle with vinegar and oil.
7. Season with salt and pepper, mix together.
8. Serve at room temp.

Taco Soup

1 lb ground beef
1 Tbsp or 1 pkg taco seasoning
1/2 tsp pepper
2 cans tomato sauce
2 cans water
1 can Rotel
1 can corn
1 can ranch style beans
1 pkg Ranch dressing
1/2 small onion, chopped
1 Tbsp butter

Directions

1. Place butter and onions in skillet and cook until tender, stirring frequently.
2. Add ground beef, taco seasoning and pepper and cook until brown.
3. Pour into a large pot.
4. Add the remixing ingredients to the pot.
5. Bring to a boil, stirring frequently.
6. Let simmer for 10 minutes.
7. Make yourself a bowl with your desired toppings. I like crushed tortilla chips and shredded cheese.

Chipotle Bacon Mac & Cheese

1.5 tsp salt
1 (16 oz) pkg. macaroni pasta
2 Tbsp corn oil
1/2 cup butter
1 small onion, diced
3 Tbsp flour
3 cups half & half
2 cups heavy cream
1 tsp ground white pepper
3 cups freshly grated smoked cheddar cheese
1 cup freshly grated cheddar cheese
1 tsp ground chipotle Chile pepper
6 cooked bacon slices, chopped
3/4 cup bread crumbs

Directions

1. Preheat oven to 350 degrees.
2. Cook pasta according to package directions.
3. Drain, then rinse with cold water and toss with 1 Tbsp of corn oil.
4. Melt butter in a large saucepan over medium-high heat.
5. Add onion and sauté 4-5 minutes until tender.
6. Add flour to saucepan and cook, whisking constantly, 1-2 minutes or until smooth.
7. Add half & half, cream, white pepper and salt and bring to a simmer.
8. Cook, whisking constantly, 5-6 minutes or until thickened.
9. Gradually add cheeses, stirring until well blended.
10. Transfer mixture to a large bowl and stir in pasta.
11. Spoon into a lightly greased 9x13 baking dish.
12. Sauté chipotle pepper in remaining 1 Tbsp corn oil in a small skillet over medium heat for 30 seconds or more until mixture begins to smoke.
13. Remove from heat and quickly stir in bacon and bread crumbs until coated.
14. Sprinkle mixture over pasta.
15. Bake for 15-20 minutes or until golden and crisp on top.

Pasta Fagioli Soup

2 lbs ground beef
1 Tbsp olive oil
1.5 cups onion, chopped
2 cups carrots, sliced thin
2 cups celery, diced
1 (28 oz) can diced tomatoes
2 cups canned red kidney beans
2 cups canned white kidney beans
2 (48 oz) cans beef broth
1 Tbsp dried oregano
2 tsp pepper
1.5 tsp tabasco sauce
3 (16 oz) jars spaghetti sauce
12 oz shell pasta
1 Tbsp + 2 tsp chopped fresh parsley

Directions

1. Sauté the beef in the oil in a large pot. I love adding garlic powder and onion powder when cooking ground beef.
2. Add onions, carrots, celery and tomatoes and simmer for about 10 minutes.
3. Drain and rinse the beans and add to the pot.
4. Add the remaining ingredients.
5. Simmer until celery and carrots are tender, about 45 minutes.

Honey Garlic Shrimp

1/3 cup honey
1/4 cup soy sauce
1 Tbsp minced garlic
1 tsp minced ginger
1 lb medium uncooked shrimp
2 tsp olive oil
Salt & pepper to taste

Directions

1. Whisk the honey, soy sauce, garlic and ginger together.
2. Place shrimp in a large gallon baggie.
3. Pour the marinade on top.
4. Leave in fridge for 1 hour.
5. Heat olive oil in skillet over medium-high heat.
6. Place shrimp in skillet.
7. Cook shrimp on one side until pink, about 45 seconds then flip over and cook shrimp for another minute.
8. Serve shrimp over rice.

Carbonara with Pan-Seared Scallops

4 large scallops per person
2 Tbsp olive oil
2 Tbsp butter
Salt & pepper to taste
8 slices thick cut bacon, diced
1 shallot, finely sliced
I clove garlic, leave whole
4 green onions
2 egg yolks
1/2 cup cream
1 cup grated Parmigiano Reggiano
14 oz linguine

Directions

1. Start cooking pasta according to box directions.
2. In a small bowl mix together cream, egg yolks and 3/4 of cheese.
3. In a large skillet, cook bacon until crisp and add shallots and 1/2 of the green onions.
4. Smash down garlic clove a bit and add to bacon.
5. Blot scallops with a paper towel to remove any water.
6. Add salt and pepper.
7. Heat frying pan and olive oil.
8. Make sure pan is hot before adding scallops.
9. Leave plenty of space in between scallops in pan.
10. You may need to cook in batches.
11. Sear for about 2-4 minutes or when bottom is a nice golden brown.
12. Peek under to see if done but don't move around.
13. Turn to sear other side, about 1-3 minutes.
14. Add butter to pan and spoon once melted over scallops.
15. When pasta is done, drain.
16. Remove the garlic from the skillet and add pasta.
17. Toss well then transfer to a large bowl.
18. Add cream mixture to pasta and combine well.
19. Make sure pasta is still hot in order to cook the eggs and melt the cheese.
20. Arrange pasta on a plate, top with scallops, grated cheese and green onions.

My Favorite Lasagna

9 lasagna noodles
1 Tbsp olive oil
1 lb ground beef
1 lb ground Italian sausage
1 tsp garlic salt
1 tsp dried oregano
1/2 tsp dried thyme
1/4 tsp dried basil
4 (15 oz) cans tomato sauce
1 (15 oz) container ricotta cheese
3 eggs, beaten
1/3 cup grated Parmesan cheese
1 lb shredded mozzarella cheese
Salt & pepper to taste

Directions

1. Preheat the oven to 350 degrees.
2. Bring a pot of lightly salted water to a boil.
3. Add the noodles and olive oil and cook for 8-10 minutes.
4. Drain the pot and set noodles to the side. I lay them out on parchment paper.
5. Cook the beef and sausage in a large pot. I love adding a little garlic and onion powder.
6. Stir in the garlic salt, oregano, thyme, basil and tomato sauce.
7. Season with salt and pepper.
8. Simmer for 30 minutes.
9. Meanwhile, mix together the ricotta cheese, eggs and Parmesan cheese in a bowl.
10. Ladle enough of the meat sauce into a 9x13 pan to cover the bottom in a thin layer.
11. Form a layer on top of the sauce with 3 noodles.
12. Spread about 1/4 of the cheese mixture over the noodles.
13. Sprinkle about 1/3 of the mozzarella cheese over the cheese mixture then ladle about 1/3 of the meat sauce over the mozzarella cheese.
14. Repeat layering twice more, topping with the remaining 1/4 lb mozzarella cheese.
15. Bake for 75 minutes.
16. Allow to sit for 10 minutes before serving.

Hey y'all, welcome to my channel...I mean OUR cookbook! I'm so excited to bring y'all a slice of my southern cooking into your home!

I'm a southerner true & true! Born & raised in Covington, Louisiana. My passion for cooking first originated from my family & then as I got older, I was obsessed with cooking shows and that inspired me to branch out more as a cook. I've been married to my best taste tester, Lonnie for 13 years. My two boys, Trey & Waylon definitely mold the way I cook which is southern, simple ingredients, effortless, and above all, darn tasty! My love of food has converted into my YouTube channel in a series I call Foodie Fridays. There, I bring a weekly recipe that meets all the Nicole Burgess criteria. It's become one of my most requested videos on my channel & most watched playlist.

I hope the recipes in this cookbook take you away to swinging on a porch swing, drinking sweet tea, & enjoying some southern decadence. Enjoy y'all! xoxo

Southern Sweet Tea

1-gallon size or 2 family size tea bags
1.5 cups white granulated sugar
Lemon for garnish

Directions

1. Bring a small pot of water to a boil.
2. Add your tea bag(s) and turn off the heat.
3. Allow the tea bag(s) to steep for 30 minutes.
4. Discard the tea bags.
5. In a large pitcher add your sugar and pour in your tea concentrate.
6. Stir well until all sugar is dissolved.
7. Add sliced lemons for flavor or garnish.
8. Place the pitcher in the refrigerator and chill.
9. Serve over ice and Enjoy!

Southern Deviled Eggs

7-8 eggs, boiled & peeled
1/4 cup mayo
1.5 Tbsp sweet pickle relish
1 tsp yellow mustard
Salt & pepper to taste
Paprika

Directions

1. Cut your eggs in half lengthwise.
2. Remove the yolks and put them in a bowl.
3. Mash the yolks with a fork and mix in the mayo, relish and mustard.
4. Add the salt and pepper.
5. Fill your empty eggs evenly with mixture.
6. Garnish with paprika.
7. Store covered in the refrigerator.

Fiesta Cups

3 packs mini filo sheets (in the freezer section)
1 can mild diced tomatoes/chilis (I recommend Rotel)
1 bag real bacon bits
1.5 cups shredded Colby & Monterrey Jack cheese
1 cup mayo
Pepper to taste

Directions

1. Preheat oven to 350 degrees.
2. In a bowl mix drained tomatoes/chilis, bacon bits and mayo until blended.
3. Add in the cheese and stir until fully incorporated.
4. Fill your shells. Don't fill up too much because you want to make sure you have enough filling for all your shells. About 1 Tbsp each.
5. Bake for 15-20 minutes or until golden and bubbly.

Big Lonnie's Taco Soup

2 onions, chopped
1 green bell pepper, chopped
2 garlic cloves, minced
3 cans kidney beans
2 cans corn
28 oz can petite diced tomatoes
1 can tomato/chilis (I suggest Rotel)
2 (15 oz) cans tomato sauce
3 packs taco seasoning
1 pkt Ranch
2 lbs ground meat
Water (I used about 5 cans)

In Memory Of

Directions

1. After chopping your veggies, sauté them in 3 Tbsp of butter until soft or the onions are opaque.
2. Add your ground meat and cook until browned.
3. Drain grease.
4. Return to pot.
5. Add all remaining ingredients and cook on low/medium heat until heated through and flavors are blended.
6. Top with sour cream, shredded cheese and corn chips.

Sweet Southern Cornbread

1 cup flour
1 cup yellow cornmeal
2/3 cup white sugar
1 tsp salt
3.5 tsp baking powder
1 egg
1 cup milk
1/3 cup vegetable oil
1/4 cup diced jalapeños (I recommend the diced jar kind)

Directions

5. Preheat your oven to 400 degrees.
6. Spray your 9-inch round cake pan with a non-stick cooking spray. I suggest Baker's Joy.
7. In a medium bowl, combine flour, cornmeal, sugar, salt and baking powder.
8. Stir in egg, milk and vegetables oil until fully combined.
9. Add your diced jalapenos and stir until fully incorporated with the mixture.
10. Pour the batter in your sprayed pan.
11. Bake for 25 minutes or until a toothpick inserted comes out clean.

Mom's Tuna Casserole

2 boxes mac & cheese (I suggest Kraft)
1 can cream of mushroom soup
1 can sweet peas, drained
1 can tuna fish, drained
Milk
Pepper

Directions

1. Cook your Mac & cheese according to the package.
2. Add cream of mushroom soup and almost a can of milk.
3. Stir and blend together.
4. Add your drained peas and tuna fish.
5. Mix together.
6. Add your pepper to taste and cook on low/medium high heat until thickened and hot.
7. This recipe is perfect for adding other ingredients as well!

Slow Cooker Whole Chicken

2 tsp salt
2 tsp paprika
1/2 tsp cayenne pepper
1 tsp onion powder
1.5 tsp black pepper
1/2 tsp garlic powder
1 whole chicken
1 white onion, chopped

Directions

1. Add all spices in a bowl and mix together.
2. Put your chopped onions in the bottom of the slow cooker.
3. Rub your spices all over your chicken.
4. Cook on low for 8 hours.

Restaurant Style Alfredo Sauce

1 lb fettuccine, cooked
1 lb of protein (I suggest shrimp)
1 Tbsp unsalted butter
3-4 cloves garlic, minced
1/2 cup heavy cream
1/2 cup whole milk
1/3 cup grated parmesan cheese
1 egg yolk, beaten
2 Tbsp parsley, chopped
Plenty of salt & pepper

Directions

1. Cook your pasta according to the package, drain.
2. Cook your protein and set aside.
3. Combine butter, garlic, heavy cream and milk in a pot over medium/high heat.
4. Bring to a simmer.
5. Remove from the heat and slowly stir in parmesan cheese and egg yolk.
6. Make sure it's cooled enough that your egg doesn't scramble.
7. Put back over low heat and constantly whisk until cheese is melted.
8. Stir in your pasta and protein.
9. Season with salt and pepper.
10. Garnish with parsley and serve immediately.

Note: I double the recipe to make enough sauce for the 1 lb of fettuccine.

Slow Cooker Red Beans

1 lb red beans
6-7 cups water
1 lb sausage
1 sweet onion, chopped
1 green bell pepper, chopped
8 cloves garlic, minced
1 tsp pepper
1 Tbsp creole seasoning (I suggest Tony Cachere's)
1 bay leaf

Directions

1. Soak your beans in water overnight.
2. Add all ingredients to the slow cooker.
3. Cook on low for 8 hours.
4. The beans will have a thin consistency but thicken up overnight.

Slow Cooker Chicken Parmesan

1 bag (26-32 oz) frozen fully cooked breaded chicken strips (I suggest Tyson's Southern Breast Tenderloins)
8 oz sliced mozzarella cheese
Italian seasoning for topping
1 slow cooker liner

Sauce Ingredients

28 oz can petite diced tomatoes
6 oz can tomato paste
3 garlic cloves, minced
1 tsp salt
1/2 tsp pepper
1 tsp oregano
1 tsp basil
2 Tbsp brown sugar

Directions

1. Place your slow cooker liner in your slow cooker.
2. Mix all your sauce ingredients in the crockpot.
3. Cover and cook on low for 2-3 hours.
4. Add your chicken tenders, making sure to cover as much as possible with the sauce.
5. Put the lid back on and cook on high for 1 hour.
6. Place your cheese on top for the last 15 minutes and allow it to melt completely.
7. Sprinkle some Italian seasoning on top.

Slow Cooker Chicken & Dumplings

4 large or 6 small chicken breasts (frozen or thawed)
2 Tbsp butter, cut in small pieces
3 (10.5 oz) cans cream of chicken soup
32 oz chicken broth
1 white onion, chopped
10 refrigerator biscuits
Garlic powder
Cajun seasoning (optional)
Poultry seasoning to taste
Salt & pepper to taste

Directions

1. Place chicken breasts in the crockpot and top with butter.
2. Season your chicken breasts with however much you prefer.
3. Chop your white onion and place on top of the seasoned chicken breasts.
4. Place your cream of chicken soup and chicken broth in a large bowl and whisk together.
5. Pour soup mixture on top of the chicken breasts making sure to cover as much as possible.
6. Place the lid on the slow cooker and cook on high 4-6 hours or low 8 hours.
7. After 8 hours on low, cut your biscuits into fourths (4 pieces per biscuit) and place in the slow cooker.
8. Cover and cook on high for 30 minutes.

Best Brownies Ever!

3/4 cup unsalted butter
2 eggs
1 cup sugar
2/3 cup light brown sugar
2 Tbsp whole milk
2 tsp vanilla extract
3/4 cup unsweetened cocoa powder
3/4 cup all-purpose flour

Chocolate Frosting

1.5 cups semi-sweet chocolate chips
1/2 cup heavy cream
1 large tube candy coated chocolate candies (I suggest mini M&Ms)

Directions

1. Preheat the oven to 350 degrees.
2. Spray a 9x9 pan with nonstick cooking spray. I suggest Baker's Joy.
3. In a bowl, melt the butter in the microwave for 1 minute.
4. In a large bowl, mix the melted butter, sugars, eggs, milk and vanilla.
5. Whisk in the cocoa powder until smooth.
6. Add the flour slowly until fully combined.
7. Spread the batter in the sprayed pan.
8. Bake for 25-30 minutes or until a toothpick comes out clean.
9. Cool completely.
10. Heat heavy cream in a medium pot.
11. Add chocolate chips and stir until melted and smooth.
12. Pour the chocolate over the brownies and smooth evenly.
13. Sprinkle with the chocolate candies.
14. Refrigerate until the chocolate has set.

Runaway Bride Bars

1 white cake mix
3 eggs
1/2 cup butter, melted
1 box powdered sugar
8 oz cream cheese, softened
4 Tbsp almond extract

Directions

1. Preheat the oven to 350 degrees.
2. Combine cake mix, 1 egg, butter and 2 Tbsp of almond extract.
3. Press into the bottom of a 9x13 pan.
4. Make sure that you press some crust up on the sides of the pan.
5. Using a mixer, mix the cream cheese until fluffy.
6. Add 2 eggs, 2 Tbsp of almond extract and box of powdered sugar. Pour over the crust mixture.
7. Bake for 40-45 minutes.
8. Let cool overnight before cutting.

Optional: You can add chopped pecans to the crust and coconut to the topping.

Banana Pudding

8 oz cream cheese, softened
14 oz condensed milk
5 oz instant vanilla pudding mix
3 cups whole milk
1 tsp vanilla extract
2 (8oz) containers of frozen whipped topping
4-6 bananas, sliced
1 box vanilla wafers

Directions

1. In a mixing bowl, beat the cream cheese until soft/fluffy.
2. Pour in the condensed milk, pudding packet, whole milk and vanilla until smooth/thickened.
3. Fold in 4 oz of the whipped topping.
4. In a 9x13 pan or trifle bowl, line the bottom with vanilla wafers.
5. Place sliced bananas on top of the wafers.
6. Spread the pudding mixture on top of the bananas.
7. Repeat layers until reaching the top.
8. Top with remaining frozen whipped topping.
9. Crush any remaining vanilla wafers and garnish the top.

Dew Drop Cake

1 box lemon cake mix
3 (4oz) lemon instant pudding mix
12 oz lemon/lime soda (I suggest Mt. Dew)
3/4 cup vegetables oil
4 eggs

Glaze

2 cups powdered sugar
4-5 Tbsp lemon/lime soda
Zest of one lime and one lemon

Directions

1. Preheat the oven to 325 degrees.
2. Spray a bundt pan with nonstick cooking spray. I suggest Baker's joy.
3. In a mixing bowl, combine the cake and pudding mix.
4. Add the soda, oil and eggs.
5. Beat with a mixer until smooth.
6. Pour the batter in the sprayed pan and cook for 45-50 minutes or until a toothpick inserted comes out clean.
7. Let cool in the pan for about 10-15 minutes.
8. Remove from the pan and let cool completely.
9. For the glaze: Whisk the powdered sugar, soda and zest until smooth. Pour all over the cake warm or cooled.

18596166R10045

Made in the USA
Lexington, KY
23 November 2018